INTRODUCTION

I've loved darts for as long as I cng up in a family home without sky sp< noughties, meant I didn't get to as I would have liked, so I had to ma January on the BBC.

I'd watch on the telly and think how great it would be to be able to play this game. I tried on numerous occasions to get into it, but alas, I was blessed with little or no natural ability so I'd throw for 10 or 15 minutes, hit nothing but the odd big 20, and conclude that I just wasn't ever going to be any good and should stick to watching it on telly. I was so bad, even though no one was watching I still felt embarrassed!

However, at some point during 2006, we got Sky Sports. Meaning I was able to watch the epic Taylor v Barney final of 2007. Since that point I've barely missed a tournament on the box. And this meant my repeated attempts to try and play the game become more and more frequent, after watching the Taylor Barney rematch of 2009, me and a friend (Adam) decided the time had come to take the game up properly. So we found a local club with an electronic scoreboard and went religiously every Monday for about 18 months and played first to 10.

To begin with, this took us all night – the first match I won 10-6 in about 2 and a half hours! But after a few months the time it was taking us was getting less and less and we could see the improvement.

In the early days, I had the better of the results, though I didn't have it all my own way. But suddenly, after we'd been going for about 4 months, he had a spell of about 15-20 weeks in which I only managed to beat him 2 or 3 times. This started to become difficult to take, however he was a dad, and I wasn't at the time, so the extra practice time I had available to put in started to pay dividends. Once I'd broke his winning streak I went on one of my own. Though the difference was, when I was losing a lot of them were in the 10-7 to 10-9 results bracket, however I was winning 10-3 and 10-4 regularly. I did have the odd 10-2, but we never played out a whitewash.

Inevitably though, after about 18 months Adam started losing interest and would miss the odd week, which soon became the odd couple of weeks, and then turned into pretty much every week. So I had to find myself some new opponents. Fortunately the pub I played pool in had a lower league darts team, so I was able to join them and go from there.

I now play for one of the top teams in my local league and love the challenge of it. However, I'm just an average player. Statistically, when I keep track practicing at home, I usually average somewhere in the region of 21-24 a dart. My greatest darting achievement to date is making the last 8 of a Riley's UK open qualifier in 2016 from a field of over 100 players, beating a couple of county players en route before getting whitewashed by the eventual winner in the quarter final.

The reason I give you this background, is that this book is aimed specifically at people like me, who just love the game and want to get better so they can keep enjoying it. I've included all the various practice routines I've found from numerous sources over the course of the last 8 years that have helped me, to save you the trouble of searching for new ones yourself. As I know from experience that it can take quite a bit of time to find a good one. I have also included my personal best scores for each game, to give you some targets to aim for!

GAME ON.........

CONTENTS

GROUPING

Warm up Routine
Time required – as long as you feel like

Let's start with a very basic warm up game, which I have seen recommended by the likes of Eric Bristow on various you tube clips, simple grouping practice.

This is suggested as a good way to begin a practice session, prior to getting started properly to help get your arm going and develop the consistency in your action.

Basically, you throw you first darts at any target you wish, but wherever it lands (even if you hit a big 12, going for treble 20), you aim your second and third darts at your first one. The aim of this is to get your arm used to following the first dart. So that when you do start hitting the treble 20 with your first dart, your arm is already programmed to follow it with the next two.

Bristow recommended a good 20-30 minutes on this, but depending on the level you intend to achieve, I'd say that once you start getting all three darts close to each other regularly you can move on to something more interesting.

10 BULLS

Warm up Routine
Time required – 2 mins plus

This is my go to warm up routine that I use to start pretty much all my practice sessions as a way to find my range before I move on to other things.

The idea of this game is that before you get into the meat of your session, you have to first hit at least 10 bulls. Counting the 25 as 1 (single bull) and the bullseye (double bull) as 2. However, you only have 30 darts, or 10 visits, to achieve the target.

If you fail to hit the 10 bulls within the 10 visits, then you must carry on until you reach a point that the number of bulls you have hit, equals the number of visits you've had. For example, if you've only hit 8 bulls with your first 10 visits, then you would need to hit 3 on your next visit (for 11 bulls in 11 visits) or 2 each with you next two visits (for 12 from 12) to complete the routine.

Generally I will hit the 10 bulls within 7 or 8 visits so it's not an issue, but it has been known for me to get miles behind. My worst ever, saw me at one stage 12 behind (for simplicity if I fail to get 10 from 10 I start counting in terms of how far behind I am, as on this occasion I got to over 60 visits and still hadn't caught up, so counting in terms of how far behind I was, psychologically at least, seemed less embarrassing and I started to catch up, so I've done that ever since.

As I say though, I've done this routine a lot, more than any of the others in the book, so my first record that I'm going to share with you as a target, is one that will test even the very best players. I have completed this challenge in the best possible 2 visits (although I didn't manage it in 5 darts). My first visit was 25, bull, 25. Then bull, bull, bull with the second. But I still consider anything 6 visits or under good going and probably still fail to get 10 from 10 about 10% of the time.

ACROSS THE BOARD

Warm up Routine
Time required – as long as you feel like

This is another good range-finding exercise to start a session with. With your three darts, you have 3 different targets spread across the whole board. I usually go with either top to bottom (double 20, Double 3, Bull), or left to right (Double 11, Double 6, Bull).

However you can go any way you like across the board, for example Double 14, Double 10, Bull or Double 18, Double 7 Bull. Or if you wish, you could go around the board and try all the combinations, but I generally stick to just the two.

(I should point out that the order you go for each target is up to you. I'll usually go for the doubles first and finish on the bull, but the order isn't important if you prefer to do it differently).

The idea obviously is to hit all 3 of your intended targets within the same visit, but if you can get to the stage where you are regularly hitting at least 1 out of three every time for a good few minutes consistently, then you're probably ready to move on to another routine.

This is good for getting used to using the whole board prior to getting into the session, as opposed to the 10 bulls game that is just focussed on the one area, so a combination of the two exercises for 10 to 15 minutes at the start of a session is a good way to get going.

THE 1000 POINT CHALLENGE

Scoring Routine
Time required – Approximately 4-8 minutes

I came up with this game myself not long after taking up the game and it is as simple as it sounds. This is a quick-fire scoring routine that is short enough to fit in even when you haven't got much time to practice.

The Challenge here is to score 1000 points in as few darts as possible. There is no requirement to finish on a double, nor is there any need to score exactly 1000. It's simple a case of scoring 1000 as quickly as you can using any part of the board just as you would in a game of 501. For example if you block the treble 20 bed, switch to 19's or 18's.

The game ends at the dart you go over the 1000 point barrier. So let's say for example you score 9 straight tons and a 60 in your first 30 darts. You then hit Treble 20 with the 31st dart and that's end of game as your score is now 1020 and you've achieved the 1000 point target in 31 darts. Now try and beat that on your next go!

This is also a good one to challenge your mates at, possibly for a few quid a time. As the aim of the game is to achieve the score in the fewest darts, throwing first is not an advantage in this game. Say for example your opponent is throwing first and achieves the 1000 points with their 38th dart, and you come to the board having scored 978 points with your first 36 darts, you can go for a 25 or bull knowing either will give you the win, having achieved the total in one dart less. However if you miss the 25, and say score a single 6, but then hit single 20 with the next dart, you have both completed the game in 38 darts so it's a tie and you have to start over!

As a target for you, my best at this particular game is 34 darts. Which equates to a 29.4 average per dart.

21 TON PLUSES

Scoring Routine
Time required – Dependant on standard. Maybe 10 minutes for high level county player, 20-25 minutes for steady pub league player but maybe up to an hour for beginners.

This is another routine focussed primarily on the main scoring section of the 20's. Though it could be adapted to fit the 19's or 18's should you wish. As the name suggests the idea of the game is to hit 21 ton plus scores in as little time as possible, with the scoring working as follows:

- 100+ = 1
- 140+ = 2
- 180 = 3

So theoretically, if you are MVG or Gary Anderson you could finish this game in 21 darts by piling in 7 straight 180's. But for the mere mortals among us, the aim is to steadily accumulate the points through a combination of all 3 scores, with maybe the odd 121, or 135 thrown in.

As a general rule, the game is played solely on the 20's, however you could adapt it to include switches to the 19's and 18's. But a score should only count if you hit a minimum of one big treble and 2 big singles. For example, you could hit single 20, block the bed and switch to 19's, hit a single and block that bed, so switch again and hit the treble 18. You've scored 93, but you could count this as 1 point scored. Whereas, say for example you hit single 20, block the bed, switch to 19's and hit treble 19, treble 7 with you next 2 darts, you've scored 98, but this is no good as you'd drifted outside your target area so this doesn't count.

If you are a beginner just starting out and find that, initially, this is taking more time than you have, another possible simplification I employ sometimes when I don't have much time, is that you can count a straight 60 as half a point. However, this is just a straight 60 and not 60+ scores, so 81's or 85's still don't count. This is because you are trying to train yourself to keep your darts straight. You can't let yourself be rewarded if one drifts. If you do then in your mind you will start to accept the odd loose dart. This will creep into your game on match day and that is what we are trying to eliminate!

Similarly, if you are including 19's and you hit single 20, single 19, treble 7, you've scored 60, but again this doesn't count as it includes a loose dart.

Can't really give you any targets here, but can say that this usually takes me between the 20-25 minutes to complete but it's all on the day. I have done it in closer to 15 minutes but it's also taken me over half an hour on a few occasions. It's not a good idea to start it if you haven't got much time, as trying to rush it towards the end can make you miss and affect your confidence next time you play. I'd stick to one of the shorter routines unless you know you have sufficient time to complete it even on a bad day (Though I'm speaking as someone who has an inner need to finish a game like this once I've started, even if it means I wind up late for where I need to be). If you're not like me in that sense, then you could simply see how far you get in the time you have. Or of course you can always lower the target, maybe to 10 for example, if time becomes an issue.

CONSECUTIVE 20'S

Scoring Routine
Time required – approximately 6-8 mins, providing you don't miss!

I found this simple but effective game while reading 'The way eye see the game', the Jamie Caven autobiography. It's very good for improving your consistency on hitting the 20's, but beware it can also be very frustrating!

The aim of the game is to try and score 1000 points on the 20's, without missing. So the basic premise is that you keep scoring on the twenties, as you would in a match, with a single 20 counting as 20, a double counting as 40 points and a treble 60. However, as soon as one dart lands outside the 20, that's game over and you have to start again!

So for example, let's say your first three darts are T20, S20, S20, you score 100. Then your next three darts are all single 20's, this is added to your total so you are now on 160. With your first dart of the next visit you bang in another treble 20, but at this point you start to get excited and the 8th dart drifts into the Single 5..... That's game over! You scored 220, better luck next time!

So as you can imagine, this can get pretty frustrating when just one slip can end a good score, making you focus on keeping straight. In many pub league games I've played in, keeping straight and finding the odd treble is usually enough to get you to the double first in most legs.

To give you a target to work towards, I've never been able to reach the 1000 point mark, my best effort at this is a meagre 640, which I think took me about 24 or 25 darts.

TREBLES FOR SHOW

Scoring Routine
Time required – Approximately 8-10 minutes

This scoring game is generally played on the 20's, but can be adapted to fit 19's or 18's as well should you wish to practice scoring on those numbers, or any other for that matter.

In this routine, you have 20 visits to the board with which to score. The aim being to pound that big treble bed! You score 5 points for every treble 20, 2 points for a single 20, and nothing for any other part of the board *(including double 20 – you don't get anything for lucky doubles in this game)*.

And it's as simple as that. As with the majority of these routines, you should make sure to record your scores and try to beat your own personal best every time.

If you hit a single 20 with every dart you would score 120. So anything above this is a reasonable target. My personal best on the 20's is 158, though surprisingly it is 165 on the 19's as I'm not normally a 19's man.

Finishing Routine
Time required – 2 – 10 minutes, Dependant on how far around the board you get

This practice game was devised by the legendary 1988 World Champion (and three time world masters champion) Bob Anderson. It's a variation on the traditional game of round the board on doubles.

You start with a score of 27, and with your first three darts, you aim all 3 at double 1. If you hit a double one, you add that score (2) to your total. If you hit 2 double ones, you add 4 to your score, or 6 if you manage to get all three darts to hit the intended target. However, if you miss with all three darts at double one, you deduct the value of the double (2) from your starting score.

Now for your second visit, you bring forward you score, be it 29, 31 or 33 if you've hit one or more double ones, or 25 if you haven't. This time, all three darts are aimed at double 2, with the same principle applying. So you add 4, 8 or 12 points to your score for 1, 2 or 3 successful darts, or deduct 4 points, if none of the 3 darts found their target.

This process is repeated, through all the doubles 3 to 20 in turn, then a final 3 are thrown for the Bull. At which point, you have to hit the bull to count as a scoring dart, otherwise you deduct 50 points from your total, which can make a huge difference to your final tally as it's at least a 100 point swing in the final visit.

The objective of the game is to get all the way around the board, finishing with as high a score as possible. However, if at any point your score reaches zero, then that is game over and you've got to go back to square (or double) one and start over.

This game is excellent doubles practice, just on your own, as it focusses your mind to try and make sure you hit at least 1 out of 3 doubles to avoid being punished, just as you could be in a match!

However, I believe this game really excels if there are a few of you. Maybe 5 or 6 team members could incorporate this as part of a pre match warm up, or play it as a post-match bit of fun, with perhaps a few coins on it if you are that way inclined? Each player then takes it in turns to throw their 3 darts at double, with their scores recorded. If any player reaches zero, they are out and have to sit out until the end of the game. However, if no one makes it all the way around without ending up with a negative score, everyone is back in to start again at double one.

This makes for some potentially entertaining, high pressure situations, for example if only one player makes it as far as the bull, but their score is only 45, for example, they have to hit a bull with 3 darts to win. I'd suggest a pound a man initially, with another pound a man every time the game gets rolled over if no one finishes. However others may choose to play £5 or £10 a man. If it's rolled over a few times and you've got 3 darts to hit a bull for a pot of a few hundred pounds, knowing all your team mates are willing you to miss and, most probably, actively trying to put you off, would you fancy it? *(Like a little taste of a hostile pdc crowd atmosphere in your own local!)*

I first came across this game on the sky sports website, through an article written by 3 time world champ John Part called 'Parts Darts', in which he detailed a few of his favourite practice routines. In his opinion, if you can get all the way round with a score of over 400, you are doing well, but the pros would be aiming for a score in excess of 600.

To give you an indication of how difficult that is, if you go around and manage to hit 1 of every double, including the bullseye, your final score will be 497. My personal best is 531, however, I've had a lot of goes at this game and you could count the amount of times I've scored over 400 on 1 hand. More often than not, I won't make it all the way round, and that's on my own with no pressure! In a group game it's even harder, though obviously the time required to play this game will need to be multiplied by the number of players. So, be warned, it's not something you can start at 8.15 if you match is due to begin at 8.30 and there are 5 or 6 of you!

ROUND THE BOARD

Finishing Routine
Time required:- Singles – 3-8 minutes, Doubles – 5-30 minutes,
Trebles – 10-60 minutes (all dependant on standard / throw speed)

Round the board, or round the world as it's sometimes known, is one of the most straight forward, but effective practice routines in darts. Making full use of the whole board meaning it's ideal for warming up, helping you to both find your range and get your arm going.

I would imagine most people who have bought this book will already be aware of this routine, so I won't spend much time on the details, though I do have a few variations that you may not have heard of, so don't go skipping this chapter just yet!

The basic premise of this game is that you, as the name suggests, go around the board in order. Starting with 1, then 2, then 3 and so on all the way to 20 (though you can carry on to the bull if you wish).

There are 4 variations on the same theme. You can go around the board on singles, doubles or trebles individually; or, if you have plenty of time on your hands, you can go for all three combined. Starting out on single one then hitting each single, double and treble in turn all the way around until you finish up with a treble 20.

Personally, I generally stick to just the singles and doubles versions, but mainly the doubles as that's the most important part of the game! Round the board singles though I find is a good warm up routine, as perhaps a further alternative way to vary how you start your practice sessions.

To give you some targets, round the board singles obviously the ultimate aim is to do this in just 20 darts (i.e. without missing), though I've never managed this. Like I say I usually attempt this as part of my warm up while I'm finding my range and usually take 25-

30 darts. Though I have on occasion spent 20 minutes or so, repeatedly trying to get all the way around without missing, but the furthest I've got is hitting the first 12. My best is to get around in 21 darts a couple of times, but that has been after missing one of the first 5 or 6 and taking any self-imposed pressure off!

My personal best on round the board doubles is 50 darts, however I'm still happy if I can get round in less than 80 darts (1 in 4 double success). Trebles I don't attempt very often, but I have got around in 68 darts once, though I am happy with anything less than 100 darts.

Now, as promised, the variations.......

Once you have mastered the traditional game of round the board, here are a few variations to make the game more difficult. I will be describing them in terms of round the board doubles, but the same principles can also be applied to the singles and trebles variations:

Miss 3 Go Back (amateur level):-

You start with the same principle of having to hit the doubles in order, however, you have a limited number of darts to hit your next target. If you don't, you fall back to the previous double. So how this works is, say with your first 3 darts you hit the double 1 at the third attempt. Therefore, just as in the original game you would approach the board with your next three, aiming at double 2. However, if you miss double 2 with all of your next three darts, you have to go back to double 1 on your next turn.

You can however gain yourself additional darts at a double by hitting the target earlier. So for example, if with your third visit, you hit the double 1 at the first attempt, you can then use your next 2 darts to throw at double 2. If you hit, you start the next visit at double 3, however if you miss, you still get the next 3 darts at double 2, as you haven't missed 3 clear at the double yet so don't have to move back.

This game can get very frustrating. The first time I tried, it took me a while to get beyond double 3, then once I did I made it all the way around to double 6, missed 3 there, then 2 minutes later found myself all the way back on double 1 again! On that occasion it took me about 45 minutes to get all the way around (I measure this in time rather than darts as I found the counting off putting), though I have since done it in around 16 minutes as a best time.

While this game is a step up in difficulty compared to the traditional round the board game, it's still child's play compared to the next two....

Hit Each Double Twice:

This is basically the same game as the original round the board on doubles, except to move on, you have to hit each double with 2 out of the 3 darts.

I was told of this variation by one of my pub league team mates, who said it was what he used to do when he was younger and had more time to practice. At the moment for me, this is a bit advanced. I've only attempted it once, and after about 35 minutes I was still stuck on double 7 and had to go out, so I packed it in and never returned to it. Though I intend to try again once I've improved my level on the 'Miss 3 go back version'.

N.B. My team mate never elaborated on how long it used to take him. So I couldn't state what a good time would be, however I wouldn't recommend this game until you are confident in your double hitting ability. Just getting around before you get fed up can be viewed as an achievement!

Miss 3 Go Back (professional level):

This game I came across on you tube, on a 'Winmau TV' video with 1995 BDO World Champ Steve 'The Bronzed Adonis' Beaton. I watched the video and thought 'Ha, I can't do that!' So I adapted it and came up with the 'amateur' version, as described above, which is better suited to my current level.

Basically, this is the same game as already described, however if you miss any double with 3 clear darts, you don't just go back to the previous double, you go right back to double 1 and start over!

I haven't even attempted this yet, however I do bear it in mind when playing my 'amateur' version. The furthest round I would have been so far before going back to the start would be to get to double 9. You'll need to be playing a very high standard, probably top level county at least, to be able to get this done regularly. Which is something I aim to do at some point in the next few years after progressing through the previous 2 versions first.

RTB: 3 DARTS PER DOUBLE

Finishing Routine
Time required:- 8-10 mins

This game is another adaptation of the traditional round the board on doubles that I've developed, but is easier to measure in terms of time and easier to track in terms of your improvement.

Basically, the aim of the game is you have one visit throwing at each double. So up to a maximum of three darts at double one, then three more at double two, and so on…. all the way to the bull. The idea being you count how many of the doubles you hit with the three darts (maximum score being 21).

If you hit the double with you first or second dart, that's end of visit in this game, so you can't use the surplus darts to aim at the next target.

An example of how it works in practice is as follows:

First visit at double one – miss, miss, hit – score is 1;
Second visit at double two – miss, miss, miss – score is still 1;
Third visit at double three – hit (1st dart – end of visit) – score is now 2;
Fourth visit at double four etc…….

Obviously the ultimate target is to hit all 21 doubles within 3 darts. Not as easy as it sounds, my current record is 15.

This routine leads on to its little brother……..

RTB: 1 DART PER DOUBLE

Finishing Routine
Time required:- 2-3 mins

This is effectively the same as the last routine, except you only get the one dart at each double, as the name suggests. So it's a good little warm up routine as it doesn't take too long, but can get frustrating if you reach double 6, 7 or beyond without hitting one. They can suddenly all start to look and feel a bit smaller!

So here your first visit will consist of one dart at double one, one dart at double two and one at double three. Regardless of whether you hit or miss you move on with your next dart. So your second visit you are going for doubles four, five and six, then seven, eight and nine and so on...

This game is useful practice for those combination finishes as you are constantly switching targets with every dart and have the added pressure of only having the one dart to hit your target.

Again the dream is to score the maximum 21 of 21. My current record stands at just 8, so I'm still a long way off!

121 UP

Finishing Routine
Time required:- as long as you can spare!

This game will improve your setup play as well as your double and combination finishing. Here you start with a score of 121, and you have 9 darts to finish the score in the conventional manor as you would in any 501 game.

For example, if with your first visit you hit a treble 20 to leave 61, but your second dart, aimed at the 25, lands just outside and in single 4 *(for those of you already thinking 'you should have gone single eleven to leave a shot at the bull on 121', as you have 9 darts to finish here, this game is best approached in the manor you would if your opponent wasn't on a finish, so it isn't always necessary to go the bull route).* You can then tidy this up with your third dart by hitting a single 17 to leave tops. You now have 6 darts to check out 40.

If you successfully check out 40 within the next 6 darts, you can then move up to the next target – 122. And you start again with 9 darts to finish from here. If you are successful again, move to 123, then 124, 125 and all the way through the finishes right up to 170.

However, here's the real killer, if at any point you fail to take out the required target within the 9 darts allowed, you have to go right back to the beginning and start at 121 again!

ery difficult game to finish, despite the fact that you may think, and would agree, that you should check out 121-170 within 9 darts, to o so 43 straight times is hard! (43 being 121 to 170 excluding bogey umbers 159, 162, 163, 165, 166, 168 and 169)

he furthest I have got is up to 143, and that was rare. I usually tumble around the low 130's even on a good day.

The beauty of this game though is its flexibility. There are many different alterations you can make so that it suits your current level better. For example, once you have been able to complete it all the way through to 170, try it again with only 6 darts at each finish!

Alternatively, if you are just starting out and are struggling to make progress with 9 darts, increase it to 12, or even 15. However a better method might be to take away the punishment for missing, so you could stick to the 9 darts per finish, but say for example you don't finish 126 in 9 darts, you could keep going at 126 until you do get it, then move on to 127. You could also pause and restart this game, so it could be something you tag on to either the beginning or end of a session for 10 minutes. So say you got as far as 135 in the last session, begin the next session from the same place and keep working your way up.

POINTS PER DOUBLE

Finishing Routine
Time required:- 8-10 mins

Another doubles practice game, utilising a points based scoring system this time, hence the name. This one is more flexible in that you can choose your own targets.

The basic premises is that you will have 20 visits to the board aiming at doubles. Generally I will aim at a specific double for this game, for example double 16, though you could also go around the doubles in order 1 to 20, or maybe have 5 visits each at 4 specific doubles (eg; 20's, 10's 16's and 8's). But there are plenty of other choices should you wish. Making this game a good way to both keep your eye in on your favourite doubles or put the work in on any that are giving you trouble.

The scoring is simple, every time you hit a double you score 5 points. If you manage to get all 3 darts on target in the same visit you score 15 points. Meaning the maximum available score from the 20 visits is 300. Once complete you can record your score and try to beat it next time!

A good target here would be 100 points (1 out of 3 doubles). My personal best is 120 points, achieved throwing all 60 darts at double 16, which equates to a double success rate of 40%.

COMBINATION FINISHING

Finishing Routine
Time required:- 15-20 mins

No matter what standard you are playing at, in close games if your opponent keeps hitting the 41-80 finishes with consistent regularity, it can wear you down, and create the impression in your mind that they aren't going to miss. Leading you to try harder and miss yourself.

If you've ever been in that situation, you'll know what I'm talking about. This game is designed to help ensure that you are the one hitting those combination shots regularly and is one of my favourites.

You start out by trying to finish 41 in three darts. If you manage it, you score a point. If not, you don't. Then you move up to 42 and try and take that out with 3 darts, then 43 and so on. I would suggest going up to 80. The main reason for this is that's the highest finish that doesn't require either a bull or a treble, so all the finishes up to that point are very achievable. Meaning whatever your level you should at least be getting to the double more often than not and you won't lose interest as easily.

If you are a more advanced player, you could go up to 100, 120, or right the way up to 170 if you wish. However I wouldn't advise you to go higher than your ability allows. As it can have a negative impact on your confidence if you are going through the motions of trying to check out ton plus finishes when your chances of hitting them are small. So if you are new to the game, you might want to just stick to the 41-60 range of one single, double finishes to start with.

Again, you can record your score and try to beat it the next time. As a benchmark for you my best is currently 26 out of 40 for the 41-80 range. I don't generally go higher for the reasons as described above.

SWITCH

Scoring and Finishing
Time required – any fixed time period you want (I would suggest either 20 or 30 minutes)

This is a routine I came across in one of the many darts coaching books written by David Kirby. It is good practice for a match as it gets you used to 'switching' between scoring and finishing on regular intervals. I also use this usually in the last 10 minutes or so before a league game once I've had a decent warm up and practiced a few doubles I'll see how many switches I can hit before a game.

The basic level of this game is as follows. You start off by trying to score on the 20's until you hit a score of 100 or more with 3 darts. Once that is achieved, you then need to move on to a specific finish, I would suggest either 40 or 32 being the main doubles you'd normally aim to finish on during a game. So with your next 3 darts, let's say you've chosen 32, you'd attempt to check this out in 3 darts. So if your first dart went in single 16, you'd go for double 8 with the next. If you fail to check out in 3 darts, or if you bust the score, then you revert back to 32 with your next 3 until you are successful.

Once you have completed both sections of the game (i.e. a ton plus score and a 32 finish), that counts as a 'switch', and you start again going for the next one.

That's the basics but this game is very flexible. For example when I play, I will go for a ton plus or what I would class as a ton 'equivalent'. What I mean by this is that you hit 2 big singles and 1 big treble within the visit. So a single 20, single 19, treble 18 (93) would be acceptable. But a treble 20, single 20, treble 5 (95) wouldn't be. Even though this is a higher score, it includes a stray dart and, as I mentioned earlier, you don't want to reward yourself for those as they'll start becoming acceptable in your sub conscious.

I will then also alter my finishes. For example after hitting the first ton plus score, I'll try and check out 32. After the next, I'll go for 40, then maybe 36, then 24, then back to 32 again and so on.

If you are a more advanced player, again there are adjustments you can make to suit your standard. For example in the scoring visit you might aim for a 140 plus (or equivalent – i.e. two big trebles, one big single), then a bigger finish. For example 52, or 60. Or even higher if you wish.

Like I said I usually use this routine pre match for varying times, and set myself individual targets based on how much time I have. I am usually happy to hit around 2 every 5 minutes. But I have once managed 11 in a 20 minute session to give you a benchmark.

TEAM PRACTICE GAMES

Hopefully so far you've found a few practice routines that you'll be able to work into your regular sessions and will help you improve your game. Now I'm going to go through a few of the practice games you can play with your mates /team before or after a match that can be fun and potentially profitable if you wanted to put a few quid in each to make it interesting......

HALF IT

Number of players: 2+
Duration: 10-12 mins for 2 players, allow maybe 3-5 minutes per player thereafter

The idea behind half it, is that all players will take turns to aim for different specified targets in turn to accumulate a score. However, if you fail to hit one of the targets, your score at that point is halved. The player with the largest score, after the last target has been thrown for, is the winner.

You can customise this game to your hearts content when it comes to setting your targets, and the number of targets you choose, but to explain I'll stick to the basics.....

I would recommend selecting about 10 different targets to give you enough to get a decent game going, while not so many as those struggling with low scores get fed up. I'd also always start with something easy to begin with. So for example, you first target may just be to get a 'high score'. In which case you would try to score as high as possible with you 3 darts and whatever you get, that will be your initial score.

I would also suggest you include a difficult target to finish. The one we use at our local is 81+. So, as with the first target, you have to score as high as possible with you 3 darts and anything you score over 81, gets added to the score. So for example if you hit 100, you get 19 added to your score. If you manage to hit 81 exactly, you score remains unchanged, but doesn't get halved, which could be crucial!

For the targets in between they could be anything. We would usually go around in turn and suggest an equal number of targets each. So say for example there are 4 of you playing, pick 2 each. The targets can be anything, but see the below list for some examples:

- Single number (for example 17)
  - So any dart hitting either the single 17, treble 17 or double 17 are totalled up and added to your score. Any darts missing the 17 do not count and if all three miss, your score is halved.
- Any double
  - So you can aim for any double, as you would in a double start leg. Any hit, you add the value of that double to your score
- Any treble
  - Same principles as the double
- Specific trebles or doubles
  - You could have to hit a certain one, for example double 3, in order to avoid halving you score
- Three different colours
  - So your three darts have to all land in different coloured segments of the board, for example a single 20 (black), Treble 19 (green) and single 17 (white) would give you a score of 94 to be added to your total. But if your last dart went into the treble 17, meaning you hit 2 greens, your score is halved. *Hint: start on the bull for this and try and*

get a red or green with your first dart to leave you just needing big singles with your last 2.

- Other colour combinations
    - For example, all three in the white, or a specific order such as black, white, black. These sound easy, but they aren't that simple when the pressure builds on the last dart. Especially if you have a score to protect!
- Any random Section of the board
    - You could aim to split the 11 for example (as in put a dart between the two 1's that make up the 11 on the outer ring), or go for the 'hole' in a number. For example trying to get a dart in the '0' of the number 10 on the outer ring. Any successful dart for a random target such as this would be given a specific point allocation at the start of the game. But we'd usually say things like this were worth 50 points per successful dart.

The beauty of this game is that, as the game goes on, halving your score gets bigger and bigger (i.e. half of a score of 400 is a much bigger penalty than halving a score of 50) so the pressure builds on the person in the lead. It's not uncommon for people to have the lowest score for most of the game, hit a couple of good scores late on and end up winning as the player who's been leading all the way through doesn't manage to get the 81+ score at the end and losses 2 or 3 hundred points, and the game!

That being said, it's a very satisfying achievement to lead all the way through a game and then get that 81+ score to finish with the pressure of knowing if you missed it, you'd lost! Especially if you get paid for your efforts!

KILLER

Number of players: Ideally 4+
Duration: Could be anything depending on your chosen format and playing standard

Killer as another game ideally suited to playing against a few mates. There are multiple different variations of this so I'll start with the basic method first;

Each player first has to be assigned a number. This could be drawn out of a hat, players could take turns to simply choose the number they would like or, my personal favourite, each player could throw a dart with their weaker hand. Then whichever number it lands in is their assigned number. Though please note, no 2 players can have the same number in the same game. So if a player hits a number that is already taken, they will have to throw again.

Once you've all been assigned a number, you'll need to write each number onto the scoreboard and assign each number an equal number of lives. I would suggest each number starting with 3 lives, however if you are of a higher standard, you may wish to increase the number of lives to perhaps 5, or even 10, to prevent the game from being over too quickly.

So to play the game, the aim is to 'kill' all three lives of each of your opponent's numbers, before your number has lost all of its lives.

Players will take it in turns to throw their three darts, and the first objective is to 'become a killer'. To do this you must hit the treble of your assigned number. So, for example there are 4 players in a game, your opponents have numbers 5, 10 and 15, while you have been assigned number 20. In order to become a killer, you must hit a treble 20. Once that's achieved, you can then start aiming at the trebles of your opponents numbers. Each one you hit, means a life coming off that number.

Of course your opponents are trying to remove your lives at the same time, so the winner is the last player with lives remaining.

There are a few quite basic tactics you need to be aware of in this game. An obvious one is that you should always try and remove the lives of your most accomplished opponents first, as they are more likely to take your lives the longer they are still in the game.

You also have to think if there are numbers together. For example if both treble 6 and treble 10 are in the game, you could go for them early on as it's a bigger target because you could hit either and remove a life from an opponent. Though beware that if both those numbers are in play, and one of them is yours, then you should wait and leave this opponents number until last because if you hit your own treble by mistake (after the initial hit needed to become a killer) then you lose a life.

As I previously mentioned there are numerous different variations of this that could significantly change the duration of the game. For example you could aim for the doubles instead of the trebles if you would prefer to practice on the doubles. You can alter the number of lives, as already mentioned, or you could alter the number of numbers assigned to each player. What I mean by this is, if there are 5 of you playing, you could each have 4 numbers. So each of the 20 numbers is in play. Meaning you get to practice on more of the board and get a much longer game. It also means that luck of the draw on the numbers isn't such a factor.

Another variation of this game is 'blind' killer. You'll need a pen and paper for this in order to write each number onto a little slip of paper. Each player then draws a number at random, and doesn't let any of the opponents know which number they have drawn.

You then have to aim at all the trebles (except for you own), as each treble has 3 lives. So once it's been hit 3 times, that number is out. But if there are only 4 of you playing, that's 16 empty numbers, so chances are early on, the majority of numbers eliminated will not have been picked by any player, but the game continues until there is only 1 player left standing.

Tip: It's vital in this game that you don't let your opponents know which number is yours until you've been eliminated, otherwise they will target you specifically.

Obviously you can still apply the same variations here as with regular killer (eg; each player drawing more than 1 number etc...), however an additional variation available here is that players that have been eliminated could become reinstated. To do this they continue to take their 3 darts in turn, but have to hit a bullseye in order to be able to draw a new number from those left remaining. So this can keep going until there are no numbers left to draw and only the players with numbers allocated at that point are still in the game and continue to take turns. Everyone else will have to sit out until the winner has been crowned.

Personally I am not a fan of this. I think a player shouldn't be able to come back in and win the game after they've been knocked out. The upside is at least you haven't got team mates sitting out for more than half the game if their number is one of the first eliminated. So some people prefer to have this chance to keep playing.

CRICKET – UK

Number of players: 2, or teams of 2+
Duration: Could be anything depending on your chosen format and playing standard

There are 2 versions of the game cricket, but I'll start with the UK version, as it is the one that more closely resembles actual cricket.

To start with once you've arranged your teams you have to decide which team is going to bat and who is going to bowl for the first 'innings'. You must then select the number of wickets that you will be playing. I'd suggest 10 wickets per innings (as you get in real cricket) however if there is a large number of you playing, or you play at a high level, you may wish to increase this number so that the game isn't over too quickly.

A player from the batting team will throw first. The objective while batting is to score as many points (runs) as possible. With anything that you score above 40, counting as a run. So for example a score of 41, would add 1 run to your total, whereas a score of 100, would add 60 runs. If you score anything less than 40, you don't get any runs for that turn.

After the first player from the batting team has thrown, the first player from the bowling team will go and try and take some wickets. To take wickets, the bowling team must aim for the bullseye. A single 25, counts as 1 wicket, with a bullseye counting as 2.

After that visit, the teams will then alternate players (just as in a standard doubles or trebles match). Once the 10th wicket is taken, the batting score is recorded and the teams switch roles, with the other team attempting to beat the total of runs scored before they run out of wickets. At the end of the game, the team with the most 'runs' is the winner.

There are a couple of other rules in this game though. Firstly, if you are batting and you go out of the board (eg: just above the double 20) into a no scoring area, that's a loss of a wicket (the equivalent of a batsman knocking his own stumps over). Secondly, if you are bowling and a dart strays outside the treble ring then that is a wide! You must add the number you hit to the batting teams runs. For example, if you hit a big 18, you add 18 runs to their score.

Again there are various different changes you can make to the format to suit your needs. You could play multiple innings and keep a running total of the runs to decide the winner; you could play an innings with more wickets, 15-20 for example; or you could also adjust the threshold for run scoring (eg: only scores above 60 count as runs).

CRICKET – US

Number of players: 2
Duration: 5-20 minutes depending on standard

The first time I was introduced to this game was by a guy in the pub where I first started playing darts. He wasn't in the darts team, so couldn't compete in a regular game of 501 and got me to play a game that he called 'Mickey Mouse'. I believe this is one of several names for this game but the 'official' name for it in the USA, where they run leagues and tournaments using this format, is Cricket.

This game is played using the numbers 15, 16, 17, 18, 19, 20 and bull. Each player has to first hit 3 of any of those numbers to 'open' them up for scoring. Once a number is open for a player, 2 things happen. The first, is that the player who has opened the number can now score on it, so say for example you open the 20's, any further 20's you hit are added to your total score. The second thing that happens, is that number is now no longer available for the opposing player to open. They now have to close that number (by hitting it 3 times themselves). Once a number is closed, it is out of the game and both players must move on to other targets. The winner of the game is the player with the highest score when all the numbers are closed.

The other point to note, is that doubles and trebles do count in this game, so say for example on your first visit you throw at the 20's and score 140. That counts as seven 20's, so the first 3 open the number, while the next 4 score, so you have scored 80 points in that visit, and the number is still open for your next visit (unless the opponent closes it on their turn).

That may seem a little bit complicated from first glance, but it is a fun game when you get in to it, so I think it is worth doing a quick trial run through for you to help you understand exactly how it works on a throw by throw basis:

1. Player 1 starts off with a straight ton on the 20's, so opens the number and scores 40 points;
   i. Player 1: 40, Player 2: 0
2. Player 2 hits a treble 20, to close the number, then switches to 19's and hits 2 singles;
   i. Player 1: 40, Player 2: 0
3. Player 1 goes for the 18's and hits 3 singles to open the number, but scores no points;
   i. Player 1: 40, Player 2: 0
4. Player 2 continues on the 19's, hitting a single and a treble with the first 2 darts, opening the number and scoring 57, then switches with the third to hit a treble 18 and close that number;
   i. Player 1: 40, Player 2: 57
5. Player 1 hits a treble 19, to close the number, then switches to 17's hitting a single then a treble, to open the number and score 17 points;
   i. Player 1: 57, Player 2: 57
6. Player 2 goes for 17's, hitting 3 singles to close the number, so now only 3 numbers remain available;
   i. Player 1: 57, Player 2: 57
7. Player 1 hits treble 15 and treble 16 with first 2 darts, then switches to the bull for the last visit and hits a 25 *(if he can open all 3 numbers, player 2 cannot score any more points in this leg, so any scoring dart would then be good enough for player 1 to win the game)*;
   i. Player 1: 57, Player 2: 57
8. Player 2 attempts to close the numbers and manages a treble 16, but can only hit 2 single 15's;
   i. Player 1: 57, Player 2: 57
9. Player 1 throws a single 15 (for security to take a points lead) with the first dart, before switching back to bulls, hitting 25 with the first dart, but missing with the second;

        i. Player 1: 72, Player 2: 57
10.   Player 2 hits single 15 to close that number, then hits back
    to back bullseyes (each counting as 2 bulls), meaning he opens
    the number and scores 25, giving him the win

Final score 72 – 82.

Hope that makes it clearer for you, and gives you some idea of the twists and turns this game can take, along with an idea as to why it is so popular across the pond.

Well, that's game shot and the match! I hope this book has been useful to you, and that whatever your standard, you've been able to pick up at least a few new ideas or routines to help keep your practice varied, interesting and, ultimately, help you improve your game.

N.B. If you have enjoyed this book, I would be grateful if you could leave a short review on amazon to help others find it more easily in future. Thanks in advance, Paul.

Printed in Great Britain
by Amazon